Baby
Beatitudes

Baby Beatitudes

A Pacifier for New and Expectant Parents

Pamela J. Brown

**Andrews McMeel
Publishing**

Kansas City

Baby Beatitudes

06 07 08 09 10 WKT 10 9 8 7 6 5 4 3 2 1

ISBN-13: 978-0-7407-5737-2
ISBN-10: 0-7407-5737-7

Library of Congress Control Number: 2005932605

www.andrewsmcmeel.com

Illustrations by David Walker
Book design by Diane Marsh

Why Baby Beatitudes? The quiet rhythm of milky breaths, the fragrance of powdery creases, the sweetness of tiny toes and plump, bread-dough legs. Someone please invent a better, more accurate, more powerful word than "love"! But since no one has, here is the reality of new parenthood: Exhausted though you are, loving this tiny soul more than you've ever loved anyone or anything makes you feel exhilarated and somehow . . . complete. Complete and grateful and graced and holy and mystical, all at the same time.

Why "Baby"? Many new mothers and fathers describe the baby simply as pure bliss. Others refer to their bundles of joy as a blessing from above. Because the word "beatitude" means a state or attitude of bliss, what better adjective to modify it than *baby*!

Why "Beatitude"? In the biblical times, a beatitude was a blessing: a short, memorable statement praising the noblest of human character, then stating the rewards, both

heavenly and earthly, that followed such virtue. In the same way, these baby beatitudes bless and affirm your new child, your parenthood, and all those who share this precious, fleeting stage of life with you.

Of course, there are moments when you long for your carefree pre-parenthood existence. There are discouraging times of doubt and frustration for parents, grandparents, or anyone caring for new life around the clock. But through it all, you're deeply aware your infant child is your greatest treasure and most extraordinary blessing.

I wrote these simple reflections to comfort and encourage you, fill your already brimming heart, and make you smile in recognition. Perhaps they'll remind you that mothers and fathers are not born but are created on the job. Most of all, may *Baby Beatitudes* help you hold tight to those priceless moments—even the ones that occur at 2 a.m.—when cradling your sleeping angel feels like a prayer.

Baby Beatitudes

*B*lessed are those babies who arrive on schedule,
for they give you your last memory of ever
being on time to anything.

Blessed are the precious moments when a baby boy
looks up at his mother and smiles.
If he's lucky, she'll remember those moments
when he's a teenager.

*B*lessed are the makers of rocking chairs.
Period.

$\mathcal{B}$lessed are the fathers of daughters, for they labor to keep the rest of the entire male world in line.

*B*lessed are the babies, for they teach us to appreciate the perfection of plump thighs!

*B*lessed is the big sister of a new baby, for now her favorite doll can babble without her even pulling a string!

*B*lessed are the mothers who make mistakes,
for they will learn to forgive their own mothers.

$\mathcal{B}$lessed is the baby with an eternal love for his blankie, for he shall develop loyalty for the ugly, unwashed, and faded in life.

$\mathcal{B}$lessed, sanctified, and sainted is the
inventor of the pacifier.

*B*lessed is the mother who strolls her toddler son to ball games *and* art galleries, for she teaches him there are no labels or limitations for either of them.

*B*lessed is the father who carries current pictures of his offspring, for he will not be made to feel lower than a slug when he unexpectedly runs into his wife's cousin, whose first word is "showmethepictures."

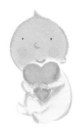

*B*lessed is the father with a quiet voice, for he will be loved at the same time he is listened to.

*B*lessed is the mother who feeds her baby on demand,
for God will do the same for her.

*B*lessed are the big brothers,
for even if they are very little, they will feel very big!

Love

*B*lessed are the mothers of ailing children,
for they will never be consumed by what is trivial.

*B*lessed are the baby's uncles, for they have studied at the University of Silly Faces and have earned their doctorate in Giving Dangerous, Inappropriate, Highly Desired Presents Forbidden by One's Parents.

*B*lessed is the doctor who enters the delivery room singing *Slip Slidin' Away* and has the presence of mind to wear gloves with traction.

*B*lessed are the parents of multiples for they shall learn to apply the rule of expansion to build extra rooms in their hearts.

*B*lessed is the mother-in-law who respects her daughter-in-law's mothering, for she will be called "Mom" instead of "Mrs. McDougal" . . . or "Hmf uh um."

Peek-a-boo!

$\mathcal{B}$lessed are laughing babies, for they repair hearts.

$\mathcal{B}$lessed are the babies who won't stay in their cribs or playpens or strollers, for they will grow up to win athletic scholarships.

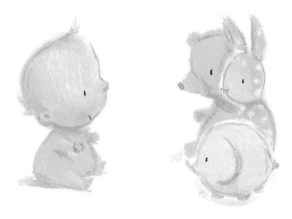

$\mathcal{B}$lessed are the sedentary, slow-moving babies, for they will grow up with matchless people skills.

$\mathcal{B}$lessed are the highly sensitive, "jumpy" babies, for they will grow up to be . . . highly sensitive.

*B*lessed is the grandfather who, although
he never learned to feed and burp his own baby,
willingly offers to get up at 2 a.m. for a night feeding
so that his *own* baby can get her rest.

$\mathcal{B}$lessed is the grandfather who never had
enough time for his own babies, for he will be the
wackiest, most-in-love, stroller-pushing,
photo-showing grandpa of all!

*B*lessed is the father who changes dirty diapers, for he will learn that men can do what women can do. Almost.

*B*lessed are the mothers who let the phone ring while singing to their babies, for they know what the human voice is truly for.

*B*lessed is the big brother, for he blazes the path that his siblings shall follow with far more permissiveness than he ever got!

*B*lessed are the babies who sleep through the night. Blessed are the babies who sleep through the night. Blessed are the babies who sleep through the night. Blessed are the babies who sleep through the night. . . .

$\mathcal{B}$lessed is the father who shares with his wife
the dream, the adoption paperwork, and the journey to
bring home their adopted child, for he will personally
experience gestation and delivery.

$\mathcal{B}$lessed is the mother with leaky nipples,
for her baby's cup runneth over.

 $\mathcal{B}$ lessed are the drooling babies,
for they show us that life is juicy!

*B*lessed are the big brothers and sisters, for they share the love and the spotlight that was once theirs alone.

$\mathcal{B}$lessed are the girl babies who come after all boys,
for they are patient with our obsession with pink.

$\mathcal{B}$lessed are the boy babies who come after all girls, for yea, though they may grow up to be poets and scholars, they are patient when we dress them in army-camouflage rompers with football appliqués.

$\mathcal{B}$lessed is the first-time grandfather, for he is married to a first-time grandmother with an eye for baby-chic and access to all his credit cards.

$\mathcal{B}$lessed are the high-maintenance babies whose demands are met with joy, for they shall grow into the least demanding, and the greatest servants, of humankind.

$\mathcal{B}$lessed is the new mother who eats the same quick, dull things every day and considers herself lucky that she even got to throw something in her mouth, for hers is the bread of commitment.

*B*lessed is the nurse who holds the mother's hand
during the pre-delivery exam, for she shall be the only
one remembered as gentle that day.

$\mathcal{B}$lessed is the father who takes his baby daughter shopping and over to watch the NFL game with his friends, for he teaches her there are no labels or limitations for either of them.

*B*lessed is the father who takes paternity leave,
for from the first day of his baby's life he will be teaching
his child what a good marriage looks like.

Blessed is the baby's young auntie, for she enjoys scrapbooking and organizing the seventy-two photos of her niece or nephew taken daily by its parents.

*B*lessed are the doctors who call to check on a sick baby's progress, for they shall never walk alone either.

$\mathcal{B}$lessed are the brothers with little sisters
and the sisters with little brothers, for they will not be
uncomfortable around the opposite sex.

$\mathcal{B}$lessed are the mothers who nap when their babies nap, for they possess the secret to postpartum happiness.

$\mathcal{B}$lessed are the pediatricians who ignore the clock during examinations, for they will merit retirements with slow ambles on the golf course and leisurely brunches.

$\mathcal{B}$lessed is the baby who is entranced with her swirling mobile, for her father may eat his dinner hot.

$\mathcal{B}$lessed are the mothers of multiples, for they shall become experts at honoring inner individuality.

$\mathcal{B}$lessed are the mothers of children with disabilities, for they will come to know God best.

*B*lessed are the fathers . . . *pant pant blow, push . . .*
who are present for the births of their children . . .
breathe, now relax . . . participate in child care . . .
now take a deep breath and puusshh . . .
toil to earn a living . . . *sorry, just a little longer . . .*
and share in the housework . . .
now bear down! That's right, puuuuuuuussssssshhhhh . . .
for it's the !$%^!*@&#%$ least they could do!

*B*lessed are the composers of lullabies.

$\mathcal{B}$lessed are the grandparents who
baby-proof what was supposed to be their
"freedom-at-last!" dream house, for neither their nest
nor their souls shall be empty.

$\mathcal{B}$lessed are the preemies, for they prove
that the bravest resides in the smallest.

*B*lessed is the father with good upper body strength, for he will ably answer the command, "Up! Up!"

$\mathcal{B}$lessed are the mothers who choose to stay home
with their babies rather than buy new kitchen wallpaper,
for their houses will be celestially decorated.

$\mathcal{B}$lessed are the mothers who choose to work outside the home, diligently doing their jobs despite leaving their hearts behind.

$\mathcal{B}$lessed is the mother who allows her baby to view her as a bank in which to deposit all hurts and worries, for she shall forever be insured against emotional bankruptcy.

$\mathcal{B}$lessed are the babies whose houses are filled with books, for they have *already* inherited the earth.

*B*lessed is the practical grandfather,
for within two hours of being told his new grandchild's
name, he establishes a tax-deferred college
savings 529 program.

$\mathcal{B}$lessed is the father who invites other little ones to play with his own, for he will learn that hosting other children means less work, not more.

$\mathcal{B}$lessed are the single mothers,
for theirs is a double portion of love.

$\mathcal{B}$lessed are the mothers who had C-sections,
for their scars are intimate reminders that they
joined God in creation.

$\mathcal{B}$lessed is the oldest sibling,
for she will become a CEO.

*B*lessed is the baby girl with an older brother,
for she will have someone to idolize, torment, hug, play
with, learn from, and stand by for the rest of her life.

$\mathcal{B}$lessed is the baby girl's big brother, for he will have someone to idolize, torment, hug, play with, learn from, and stand by for the rest of his life.

*B*lessed is the mother who must make money at home *while* caring for her babies, for the Cirque du Soleil jugglers will envy her form.

*B*lessed are the mothers with dusty furniture,
for their babies' gurgles are what get polished.

*B*lessed are the parents who understand that the books defining "normal" stages of development are not read by their babies.

$\mathcal{B}$lessed are the babies who mess their diapers just as we are leaving the house with them, for it is a sign that nurturing respects not the day planner.

*B*lessed are the mothers who give birth without
anesthesia, even though they monopolize
all the angels to do so.

$\mathcal{B}$lessed is the father who does not stint on piggyback rides, for in his old age his children will hold him up.

$\mathcal{B}$lessed is the daddy who behaves like he wants
his baby to, for he understands that his child will one day
forget his words but follow his steps.

$\mathcal{B}$lessed are all the older siblings of younger siblings, for they are able to witness the raising of the best friends they will ever have.

$\mathcal{B}$lessed is the young uncle, for he is as childlike as the babies and will entertain them ceaselessly.

 $\mathcal{B}$ lessed is the ob-gyn who says, "No apology necessary, I was awake, really." For she has strictly kept the commandment that reads, "Thou shalt not lie, unless it is the middle of the night and you practice obstetrics."

$\mathcal{B}$lessed are the babies,
for they are our models of perfect trust.

Blessed is the baby who is allowed to believe in the Tooth Fairy, Santa Claus, and the Easter Bunny, for he will grow to understand that teeth, toys, and jelly beans are never permanent but the love behind them is.

$\mathcal{B}$lessed is the mother who feeds her baby
and realizes that she is receiving as much nourishment
from the baby as she is giving.

$\mathscr{B}$lessed is the doctor who doesn't tell a mother
when to stop breast-feeding, for he knows
that it is not his business.

*B*lessed and valued above rubies is the baby's aunt,
for when you "let" her babysit she acts
like *you're* doing *her* a favor.

*B*lessed is the mother who is able to nurse gracefully in public, for she shall show the nation's Olympic gymnastic team what true agility is.

*B*lessed is the mommy who organizes a playgroup, for she shall be called Chosen Among All Mommies.

$\mathcal{B}$lessed is the baby who can't self-distract,
for we will learn our shapes and colors all over again!

$\mathcal{B}$lessed is the baby who pats back when he
or she is patted, for it teaches us we are raising
our grandchildren's parents.

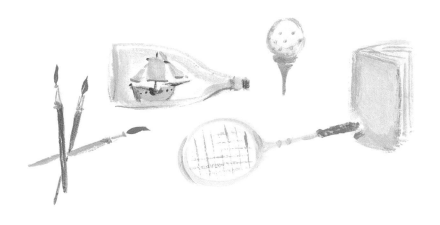

$\mathcal{B}$lessed is the father with a hobby,
for his offspring will have something to give him
other than a thousand hideous ties.

$\mathcal{B}$lessed are the colicky and "fussy" babies who must be endlessly walked, for they are the clearest lesson that most stuff in our lives can be left unattended, yet all will be well.

*B*lessed are the grandparents who have a spare room, a second home, a time-share, a summer rental, or a few extra bucks for a hotel room, for their grandchildren's parents will be eternally, annually, and obsequiously grateful.

$\mathcal{B}$lessed is the pediatric nurse who attends to the crying baby before checking parental paperwork and insurance, for she will likewise be ushered into Heaven.

$\mathscr{B}$lessed is the father of toilet-trained sons, because he has no excuse to get out of public bathroom duty.

$\mathcal{B}$lessed is the baby eating his toes,
for the Bolshoi is not that talented.

Blessed is the mother who refuses to compare her baby with other babies, for she understands that child rearing is not a competitive sport.

$\mathcal{B}$lessed are the authors of juicy romance novels, for they shall heat up the cold midnight hours of nursing mothers.

$\mathcal{B}$ lessed are the parents who are better models than critics, for their baby will learn to dance and not to duck.

$\mathcal{B}$lessed are our babies, for they allow us to love another as we are loved by God.

*B*lessed are the aunts and uncles and godparents who take their sacred jobs seriously, for their nieces and nephews and godchildren will have lifelong, built-in mentors and champions.

$\mathcal{B}$lessed are the teething babies, for in their
innocence they assure us that suffering is not sent
to us because we are "bad."

$\mathcal{B}$lessed among women is the pediatrician who has raised children heself, for she knows the parents are as much her patients as the babies.

*B*lessed is the grandmother who appreciates the miracle of both the new baby and the renewed relationship with her own child.

$\mathcal{B}$lessed are babies, for they make us grow up.
Finally.

Love

Blessed are all families, friends, and communities
who understand that babies and children are our
ultimate blessing, for theirs is the healing of the world,
and the humanity, and the glory, forever and ever, amen.